Maths Practice Year 2

Question Book

Sarah-Anne Fernandes

Name _____

Schofield&Sims

Introduction

The **Schofield & Sims Maths Practice Year 2 Question Book** uses step-by-step practice to develop children's understanding of key mathematical concepts. It covers every Year 2 objective in the 2014 National Curriculum programme of study.

The structure

This book is split into units, which are based on the key areas of the maths curriculum for Year 2. These are:

- Number and place value
- Calculation
- Fractions
- Measurement
- Geometry
- Statistics.

Each double-page spread follows a consistent 'Practise', 'Extend' and 'Apply' sequence designed to deepen and reinforce learning. Each objective also includes a 'Remember' box that reminds children of the key information needed to help answer the questions.

At the back of the book, there is a 'Final practice' section. Here, mixed questions are used to check children's understanding of the knowledge and skills acquired throughout the book and identify any areas that need to be revisited.

A mastery approach

The **Primary Practice Maths** series follows a knowledge-based mastery approach. Children deepen their learning by applying and representing their knowledge and skills in multiple ways. This approach reinforces number concepts, nurtures fluency and strengthens both reasoning and problem-solving skills. Integral to this approach is the use of visual representations of mathematical concepts. Some of the most common visual representations used in this book are:

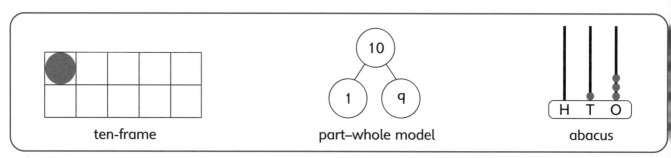

ten-frame   part–whole model   abacus

Assessment and checking progress

A 'Final practice' section is provided at the end of this book to check progress against the Year 2 maths objectives. Children are given a target time of 40 minutes to complete this section, which is marked out of 30. Once complete, it enables them to assess their new knowledge and skills independently and to see the areas where they might need more practice.

Online answers

Answers for every question in the book are available to download from the **Schofield & Sims** website. The answers are accompanied by detailed explanations where helpful. There is also a progress chart, allowing children to track their learning as they complete each set of questions, and an editable certificate.

Contents

Counting in steps of 2, 3, 5 and 10

Remember

Keep the difference between two numbers the same when counting in steps. For example: when counting in a step size of 2, the difference between each number in the sequence will always be 2.

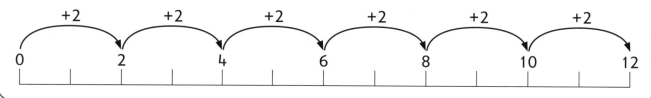

Practise

(1) Write the missing numbers on the number tracks.

a.

2	4	6			

b.

3	6	9			

c.

5	10	15			

d.

10	20	30			

(2) Write the missing numbers on the number lines.

a.

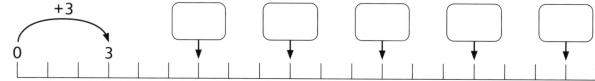

b.

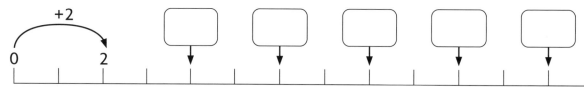

c.

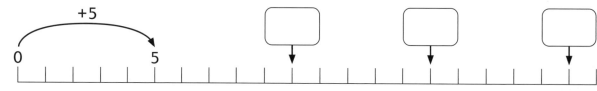

3 Grace and Ava are counting.

   a. Circle all the numbers that they will say when counting in twos from zero.

0	11	2	18	4	5	1

17	22	30	27	15	10	6

   b. Circle all the numbers that they will say when counting in threes from zero.

0	14	3	18	7	6	19

15	9	30	21	33	12	24

4 Write the missing numbers on the number tracks.

a.

20		40	50		

b.

34			64		84

c.

		72		92	

 Apply

5 Find the missing numbers by counting forwards or backwards in steps.

Count in steps of 2

   a. **A** is _____

   b. **B** is _____

   c. **C** is _____

	A
	44
	46

Count in steps of 3 →

45	B	51	C

Numerals and words

Remember

When reading and writing numbers in numerals and words, it helps to partition each number. A two-digit number is made up of tens and ones. For example: 45 = 4 tens + 5 ones = 40 + 5. This number is written as forty-five.

Practise

 1 Draw lines to match each abacus to the number written in words.

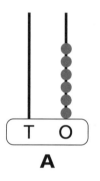 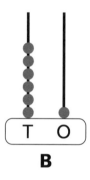 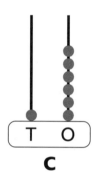 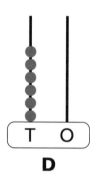

| T O | T O | T O | T O |
| **A** | **B** | **C** | **D** |

sixty   sixteen   sixty-one   six

2 Draw counters to show each number on the place value chart. Then write the number in words. One has been done for you.

a. 32

Tens	Ones
● ● ●	● ●

_____thirty-two_____

b. 63

Tens	Ones

_____

c. 16

Tens	Ones

_____

d. 75

Tens	Ones

_____

» Extend

3 Write the numbers shown by the place value counters using numerals.

a. 10 10
1 1 1 1

_____

b. 10 10 10 10 10
1 1 1 1 1 1 1 1 1

_____

c. 10 10 10 10 10 10 10
1 1 1 1 1

_____

d. 10 10 10 10 10 10
1 1

_____

Tip Numerals use the digits 0, 1, 2, 3, 4, 5, 6, 7, 8 and 9.

4 Complete the table to show these words and numerals.

	Words	Numerals
a.	nineteen	
b.		82
c.	fifty-seven	
d.		44
e.	seventy	

Apply

5 Zoe lives at house number 71. She has this plaque made with her house number written in words. The plaque is **not** correct. Explain why.

Seventeen

_____

_____

Place value and representing numbers

Remember

Every digit in a number has a value according to its position.

For example: 74 = 7 tens + 4 ones = 70 + 4

A number can be represented in many different ways, such as on a ten-frame, a part–whole model, a number line, a place value chart or an abacus.

Practise

(1) Write the number shown by the place value counters.

a. 10 10 10 10
1 1 1 1 1 1 _____

b. 10 10 10 10 10 10
1 1 1 1 1 _____

c. 10 10 10 10 10
1 1 1 _____

d. 10 10 10
1 1 1 1 1 1 _____

(2) Write the number shown by each abacus.

a.
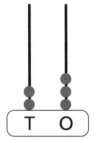
T O _____

b.
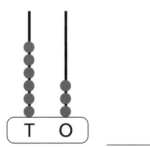
T O _____

(3) Complete the whole for each part–whole model.

a.
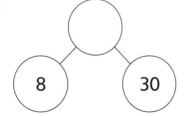

b.
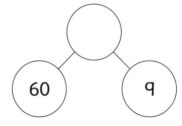

Tip Find the whole at the top of the part–whole model by adding together the parts at the bottom.

Extend

4 Draw the missing counters on the place value charts to show each two-digit number.

a. 58

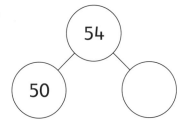

Tens	Ones
10 10 10 10 10	

b. 23

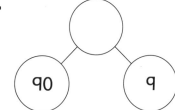

Tens	Ones
	1 1 1

5 Complete the part–whole models.

a.

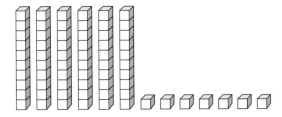

54

50

b.

90   9

Apply

6 Darcie represents the number 67 like this:

Jake represents the same number like this:

10 10 10 10 10 10
1 1 1 1 1 1 1

Who has represented the number correctly? Circle **one**.

Darcie   Jake   Both

Explain your answer.

_____

Comparing and ordering numbers

 Practise

1 Here are some sets of numbers shown using place value counters. Use the letters to order them from largest to smallest.

| 10 | 10 | 10 | 10 |
| 1 | 1 | 1 | 1 | 1 | 1 |

A

| 10 | 10 | 10 | 10 |
| 1 | 1 |

B

| 10 | 10 | 10 | 10 | 10 |
| 1 |

C

2 Circle the larger number in each pair.

a. 56 and 64   **b.** 89 and 81   **c.** 23 and 19

d. 78 and 74   **e.** 54 and 45   **f.** 33 and 30

3 Write the correct symbol (< or >) in the circle to compare the numbers.

a. 17 ◯ 21   **b.** 43 ◯ 25   **c.** 92 ◯ 34

d. 54 ◯ 57   **e.** 81 ◯ 80   **f.** 23 ◯ 27

g. 38 ◯ 35   **h.** 67 ◯ 89   **i.** 25 ◯ 15

Tip The symbol > means 'greater than' and the symbol < means 'less than'.

Extend

4 Write these numbers in the correct position on the number line.

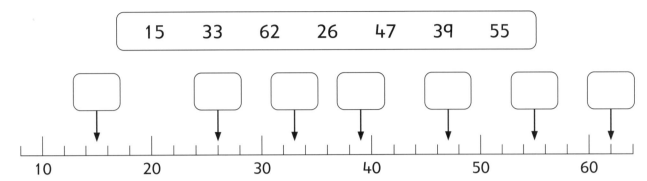

15   33   62   26   47   39   55

5 Write these numbers in order from lowest to highest.

a. 37   49   32   41   40

_____

b. 98   56   52   76   71

_____

c. 34   87   31   79   83

_____

 Apply

6 Tom says that 39 is larger than 40 because it uses the digit 9. Tom is **not** correct. Explain why.

_____

_____

7 Naomi has four number cards. She makes a number that is larger than 30 but smaller than 50. What could Naomi's number be? List **six** possible numbers.

3   4   1   5

_____

Mental addition and subtraction to 20

Remember

Using number bonds to 10 can help with addition and subtraction facts to 20.
For example: 14 + 6

14 is 10 + 4. 4 + 6 is a number bond to 10. 10 + 10 = 20. So, 14 + 6 = 20.

Number bonds to 10 that are essential to learn are:

0 + 10 = 10   1 + 9 = 10   2 + 8 = 10
3 + 7 = 10   4 + 6 = 10   5 + 5 = 10

Practise

(1) Complete these calculations using the number lines.

```
|  |  |  |  |  |  |  |  |  |  |  |  |  |  |  |  |  |  |  |  |
0  1  2  3  4  5  6  7  8  9  10 11 12 13 14 15 16 17 18 19 20
```

a. 11 + 9 = _____

b. 15 + 5 = _____

c. 7 + 13 = _____

d. 18 + 2 = _____

(2) Complete the calculations using the ten-frames.

a.

12 + _____ = 20

b.

16 + _____ = 20

c.

9 + _____ = 20

d.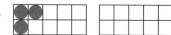

3 + _____ = 20

(3) Complete these part–whole models.

a.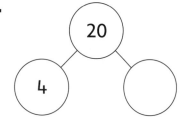

20

4

b.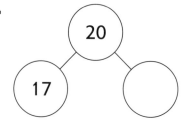

20

17

Extend

4 Draw lines to match the numbers that total 20.

13		8
15		1
12		7
19		5
14		6

Tip Number bonds to ten will help you work out these number bonds to twenty.

5 Complete the number statement. Give **four** different answers. Each card can only be used once in each number statement.

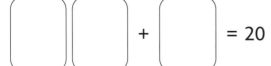

| 0 | 1 | 2 | 3 | 4 | 5 | 6 | 7 | 8 | 9 |

☐☐ + ☐ = 20   ☐☐ + ☐ = 20

☐☐ + ☐ = 20   ☐☐ + ☐ = 20

Apply

6 Lily bakes some cupcakes. 11 cupcakes have chocolate icing. 3 cupcakes have strawberry icing. 6 cupcakes have no icing. How many cupcakes are there altogether? _____

7 Tim sold 6 bikes over the weekend. He had 20 bikes in stock at the beginning of the weekend. How many bikes does he have in stock now? _____

Mental addition and subtraction to 100

Remember

Using number bonds to 10 can help with addition and subtraction facts to 100.

For example: 8 + 2 = 10 so 80 + 20 = 100.

Number bonds to 100 that are essential to learn are:

0 + 100 = 100	10 + 90 = 100	20 + 80 = 100
30 + 70 = 100	40 + 60 = 100	50 + 50 = 100

 ## Practise

(1) Draw the missing place value counters to make 100.

a.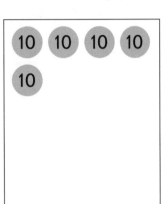

b.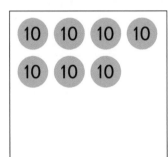

c.

(2) Complete these part–whole models.

a.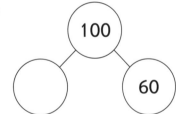

b.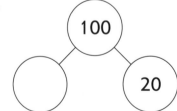

c.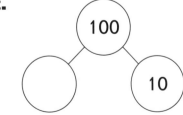

d.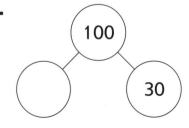

Tip Subtract the part at the bottom of the model from the whole at the top to find the missing part.

Extend

3 Draw lines to match each ten-frame to the correct number statement.

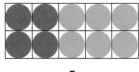 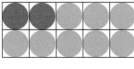 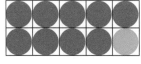 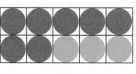

A   B   C   D

70 + 30 = 100   20 + 80 = 100   40 + 60 = 100   90 + 10 = 100

4 Write the missing numbers on the bar models.

a.

100	
35	

b.

100	
46	

c.

100	
17	

d.

100	
82	

Tip Remember that the numbers in the bottom bars should total the number in the top bar.

Apply

5 Solve these problems.

a. Alice and Nasim have some football cards. Alice has 24 cards. Nasim has 76 cards. How many football cards do they have altogether? _____

b. Lucas plants some bulbs. 45 bulbs are tulips. 55 bulbs are snowdrops. Calculate the total number of bulbs planted. _____

Addition in columns

When adding numbers with up to two digits, set the numbers into columns. First, add the ones digits, then the tens digits. Sometimes it is necessary to exchange 10 ones for 1 ten or 10 tens for 1 hundred. To estimate an answer, round the numbers before doing the calculation. Check the answer using the inverse (opposite) operation. The inverse operation of addition is subtraction.

```
    4  5
 +  3  2
 ───────
    7  7
 ───────
```

Practise

(1) Draw place value counters to complete the calculation. Then write the answer in digits. One has been done for you.

a. 14 + 12 = __26__

Tens	Ones
10	1 1 1 1
10	1 1
10 10	1 1 1 1 1 1

b. 34 + 25 = _____

Tens	Ones
10 10 10	1 1 1 1
10 10	1 1 1 1 1

c. 43 + 24 = _____

Tens	Ones
10 10 10 10	1 1 1
10 10	1 1 1 1

d. 54 + 28 = _____

Tens	Ones
10 10 10 10 10	1 1 1 1
10 10	1 1 1 1 1
	1 1 1

Extend

2 Estimate, calculate and check the answer to each calculation using the expanded column method. One has been done for you.

a.

$$
\begin{array}{r}
50 + 3 \\
+ \quad 10 + 4 \\
\hline
60 + 7
\end{array} = \underline{67}
$$

b.

$$
\begin{array}{r}
30 + 7 \\
+ \quad 50 + 8 \\
\hline

\end{array} = \underline{}
$$

3 Estimate, calculate and check the answer to each calculation using the formal column method.

a.

$$
\begin{array}{r}
2\ 5 \\
+\ 3\ 3 \\
\hline

\end{array}
$$

b.

$$
\begin{array}{r}
5\ 4 \\
+\ 3\ 8 \\
\hline

\end{array}
$$

4 Complete these calculations using the expanded or formal column method.

a. 27 + 37 = _____

b. 83 + 56 = _____

Apply

5 Solve these problems.

a. There are 34 footballs and 23 rugby balls in the cupboard. How many balls are there altogether? _____

b. Remi buys a T-shirt and pair of jeans. The T-shirt cost £16. The jeans cost £39. What is the total cost of both items? _____

c. There are 54 taxis at the taxi station during the day. In the evening, the number of taxis increases by 17. How many taxis are now at the taxi station? _____

Tip The words 'altogether', 'total' and 'increase' are mathematical vocabulary used for addition calculations.

Subtraction in columns

Practise

1 Cross off the place value counters to subtract the numbers and draw any exchanged counters needed. Then write the answer in digits. One has been done for you.

a. 73 − 42 = ___31___

Tens	Ones
10 10 10 10̸ 10̸ 10̸ 10̸	1 1̸ 1̸

b. 84 − 32 = _____

Tens	Ones
10 10 10 10 10 10 10 10	1 1 1 1

c. 95 − 52 = _____

Tens	Ones
10 10 10 10 10 10 10 10 10	1 1 1 1 1

d. 68 − 24 = _____

Tens	Ones
10 10 10 10 10 10	1 1 1 1 1 1 1 1

e. 73 − 38 = _____

Tens	Ones
10 10 10 10 10 10 10	1 1 1

f. 43 − 26 = _____

Tens	Ones
10 10 10 10	1 1 1

Extend

2 Estimate, calculate and check the answer to each calculation using the expanded column method. One has been done for you.

a.
$$\begin{array}{r} 40 + 8 \\ - \quad 10 + 5 \\ \hline 30 + 3 \end{array} = 33$$

b.
$$\begin{array}{r} 50 + 4 \\ - \quad 30 + 6 \\ \hline \end{array} = \underline{\quad}$$

3 Estimate, calculate and check the answer to each calculation using the formal column method.

a.
$$\begin{array}{r} 9\ 6 \\ - \ 4\ 2 \\ \hline \\ \hline \end{array}$$

b.
$$\begin{array}{r} 8\ 5 \\ - \ 3\ 5 \\ \hline \\ \hline \end{array}$$

4 Complete these calculations using the expanded or formal column method.

a. 56 − 32 = _____

b. 61 − 37 = _____

 Apply

5 Solve these problems.

a. The length of a piece of string is 67cm. Ella cuts off 35cm of string. How much string is left? _____

b. The cost of a pair of trainers is £45. The trainers are reduced by £17. What is the new cost of the trainers? _____

c. The table shows the heights of two sunflowers.

Jessie's sunflower	Ben's sunflower
93cm	68cm

Calculate the difference between the heights of the sunflowers. _____

Addition and subtraction word problems

Remember

When solving problems, read the question carefully and follow these steps. First, decide which operations to use. Next, decide if it is a one-step or two-step problem. Then complete the calculations.

These words can all be used to mean 'add': 'total', 'altogether', 'increase', 'plus', 'sum', 'and' and 'more'. These words can all be used to mean 'subtract': 'take', 'left', 'decrease', 'reduce', 'minus', 'fewer' and 'difference between'.

Practise

1 Solve these problems.

a. There are 48 books on a shelf. 3 more books are put on the shelf. How many books are now on the shelf? _____

b. The cost of a train ticket to London is £19. Next year the cost of a train ticket will increase by £4. What is the new cost of the train ticket? _____

c. 35 sandwiches are put out on a tray. After everyone has eaten, 7 sandwiches are left. How many sandwiches were eaten? _____

d. The temperature in the daytime is 24°C. It decreases by 6°C in the evening. What is the temperature in the evening? _____

e. I have 25 felt pens. Myra takes 8 of my felt pens. How many felt pens do I have left? _____

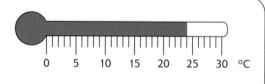

Extend

2 Solve these problems.

> **a.** Ethan scores 45 marks in his first maths test. He scores 32 marks in his second maths tests. Calculate the sum of Ethan's score for both maths tests. _____

> **b.** Seren builds a tower with 57 blocks. Jack builds a tower with 32 fewer blocks. How many blocks does Jack use to build his tower? _____

> **c.** There are 56 tins of chicken soup and 48 tins of tomato soup. How many more tins of chicken soup than tomato soup are there? _____

 Apply

3 Solve these problems.

> **a.** Skye is playing a dice game. She has rolled a total score so far of 27.
>
> She rolls the dice again and gets and . What is her new total score? _____

> **b.** Kim and Raj are skipping. Raj does 38 skips. Kim does 14 more skips than Raj. How many skips do they do altogether? _____

> **c.** A bus has 65 seats. 20 seats are empty. 7 people get off the bus. How many seats are now empty? _____

> **d.** Bindi is 23 years old. Sam is 9 years older than Bindi. What is the total of their ages? _____

Two times table

Remember

Numbers can be multiplied and divided without a written method. This is called mental calculation.

Learning the two times table helps with remembering multiplication facts quickly. Multiplication facts can help with division facts because they are opposites (inverse). For example: $2 \times 5 = 10$ so $10 \div 2 = 5$.

 Practise

1 Count in twos.

a. How many boots are there?

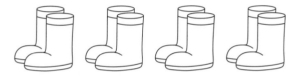

_____

b. How many wheels are there?

_____

c. How much money is there in total?

_____

2 Complete the multiplication facts using the arrays.

a.

2 × _____ = _____

b. ●●●●●●●●●●
●●●●●●●●●●

2 × _____ = _____

c. ●●●
●●●

2 × _____ = _____

d. ●●●●●●●●●●●●
●●●●●●●●●●●●

2 × _____ = _____

3 Write the missing numbers to complete the multiplication grid. One has been done for you.

×	3	4		6	7	
2	6	8	10			16

4 Complete the calculations using the two times table.

a. 9 × 2 = _____

b. 12 × 2 = _____

c. 2 × 2 = _____

d. 2 × 0 = _____

e. 16 ÷ 2 = _____

f. 10 ÷ 2 = _____

g. 22 ÷ 2 = _____

h. 14 ÷ 2 = _____

i. 8 × _____ = 16

j. 1 × _____ = 2

k. _____ = 2 × 5

l. _____ = 6 ÷ 2

 Apply

5 Solve these problems.

a. Jenny has six pairs of socks. How many socks does she have in total?

_____

Tip A pair is equal to two things. For example: a pair of shoes is two shoes.

b. There are two chairs at each desk. How many chairs are there at 9 desks?

_____

c. Dan has 10 football cards. He shares them equally with Umar. How many football cards do they each get?

_____

Five times table

 Practise

(1) Count in fives.

a. How many fingers are there?

 _____

b. How many arms are there?

 _____

c. How much money is there in total?

 _____

(2) Complete the multiplication facts using the arrays.

a.

5 × _____ = _____

b.

•••••

5 × _____ = _____

c.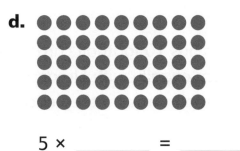

5 × _____ = _____

d. ••••••••••
•••••••••
•••••••••
•••••••••
•••••••••

5 × _____ = _____

Extend

3 Complete the calculations using the five times table.

a. $5 \times 10 =$ _____

b. $12 \times 5 =$ _____

c. $5 \times 9 =$ _____

d. $5 \times 0 =$ _____

e. $25 \div 5 =$ _____

f. $30 \div 5 =$ _____

g. $40 \div 5 =$ _____

h. $15 \div 5 =$ _____

i. $4 \times$ _____ $= 20$

j. $7 \times$ _____ $= 35$

k. _____ $= 11 \times 5$

l. _____ $= 60 \div 5$

4 Write **four** different calculations for the multiplication and division triangle. One has been done for you.

a. __5__ $\times$ __9__ $= 45$

b. _____ $\times$ _____ $= 45$

c. $45 \div$ _____ $=$ _____

d. $45 \div$ _____ $=$ _____

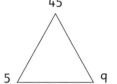

Apply

5 Solve these problems.

a. There are five players in each football team. How many players are there in 5 teams?

_____

b. There are 15 cupcakes. They are packed in boxes of 5. How many boxes of cupcakes are there?

_____

Ten times table

 Practise

(1) Count in tens.

a. How much money is there in total?

_____

b. How many eggs are there?

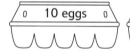 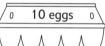 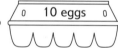 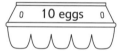 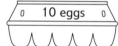

_____

(2) Complete the multiplication facts using the arrays.

a.

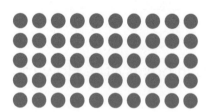

10 × _____ = _____

b.

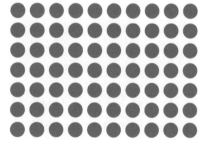

10 × _____ = _____

c.

10 × _____ = _____

d.

10 × _____ = _____

Extend

3 Write the missing numbers to complete the multiplication grid. One has been done for you.

×	5	6	7		9	
10	50	60		80		100

4 Complete the calculations using the ten times table.

a. $2 \times 10 = $ _____

b. $12 \times 10 = $ _____

c. $1 \times 10 = $ _____

d. $10 \times 0 = $ _____

e. $40 \div 10 = $ _____

f. $90 \div 10 = $ _____

g. $70 \div 10 = $ _____

h. $110 \div 10 = $ _____

i. $7 \times $ _____ $ = 70$

j. $10 \times $ _____ $ = 80$

k. _____ $ = 10 \times 10$

l. _____ $ = 100 \div 10$

Apply

5 Solve these problems.

a. The school hall is 10 metres long. Class 2B runs the length of the hall 7 times. How many metres have they run?

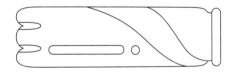

10m

_____

> **Tip** Length is the distance from one end of something to the other end.

b. There are 3 tennis balls in a tube. How many balls are in 10 tubes?

_____

c. There are 70 stickers in a pack. 10 stickers are put on each sheet. How many sheets are in the pack?

_____

Multiplication and division word problems

Remember

When solving problems, read the question carefully and follow these steps. First, decide which operations to use. Next, decide if it is a one-step or two-step problem. Then complete the calculations.

There are different words that can be used for multiplication and division word problems. These words can all be used to mean 'multiply': 'product', 'times', 'double', 'lots of' and 'groups of'. These words can all be used to mean 'divide': 'group', 'half' and 'share equally'.

Practise

1 Solve these problems.

> **a.** There are 14 seeds. The seeds are shared equally between two pots. How many seeds are in each pot?
>
> _____
>
>

> **b.** A shop sells half of these cookies. How many cookies are sold?
>
> _____
>
>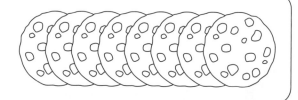

> **c.** A ticket costs £10. How much does it cost to buy four tickets?
>
> _____
>
>

> **d.** There are 6 pairs of trainers. How many trainers are there in total?
>
> _____
>
>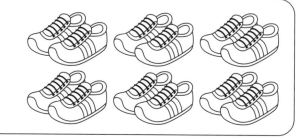

Extend

2 Solve these problems.

a. Mia draws a 12cm line.
12cm

Zack draws a line that is double the length of
Mia's line. What is the length of Zack's line? _____

b. Liam rolls 4 on his die.   Theo rolls 5 on his die.

Calculate the product of Liam and Theo's dice. _____

c. A ladybird has 7 spots. How many
spots do 5 of these ladybirds have? _____

 Apply

3 Solve these problems.

a. Ellis has 3 packs of cards. Each pack
of cards has 10 cards. Ben has 2
packs of cards. Each pack of cards
has 5 cards. How many more cards
does Ellis have than Ben? _____

b. A party shop sells balloons in packs
of 10 balloons. Kemi needs 42
balloons. How many packs of
balloons does she need to buy? _____

Recognising fractions

Remember

A fraction is part of a whole, which might be a shape, a number or a quantity. When a number, shape or quantity is divided into fractions, each part must be the same size (equal).

A half is one of two equal parts. Half of these pencils are shaded:

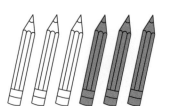

A quarter is one of four equal parts. The cake has been cut into quarters:

A third is one of three equal parts. A third of the bar has been shaded:

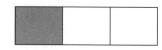

Practise

1. Shade half of each shape. Use the dashed lines to help.

a.
b.
c.

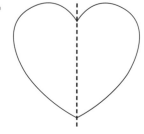
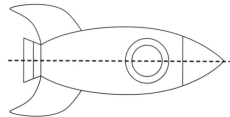
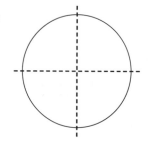

2. Write the fraction of each set that is circled.

a.

_____

b.

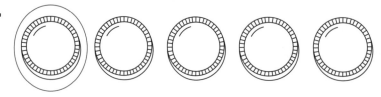

_____

3 Write the fraction of each shape that is shaded.

a.  _____

b.  _____

c.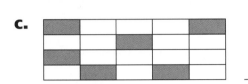

_____

d.  _____

4 Here are some fraction bars.

a. Circle the letter of the bar that is cut in half.

A   **B**   **C**

b. Circle the letter of the bar that is cut into quarters.

A   **B**   **C**

 **Apply**

5 Lucy is making a flower. Each flower is made of 4 parts:

How many whole flowers can be made from these parts?

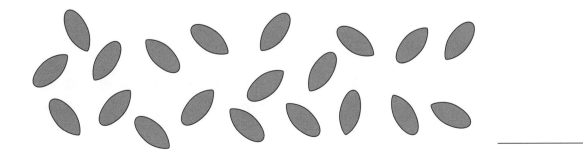

_____

Finding fractions of a number

Remember

A fraction is part of a whole. To find a fraction of a number or quantity, divide the whole by the denominator (the bottom number) to find one equal part. For example: $6 \div 2 = 3$ so $\frac{1}{2}$ of 6 is 3.

Practise

1   **a.** Draw a line to divide each picture in half.

  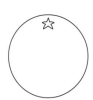

     b. Draw lines to divide each picture into quarters.

  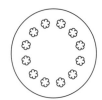

2   Find the fraction of each amount.

     a. Circle $\frac{1}{2}$ of the marbles.

     b. Circle $\frac{1}{3}$ of the pens.

3   Use the bar diagrams to find the fractions of 16.

     a. 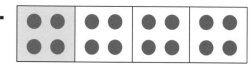   **b.**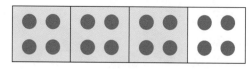

     $\frac{1}{4}$ of 16 = _____ $\frac{3}{4}$ of 16 = _____

4 Draw the counters in the circles to find these fractions.

a. Share the counters equally between two groups to find half of 12.

○ ○ ____

b. Share the counters equally between four groups to find a quarter of 12.

○ ○ ○ ○ ____

c. Share the counters equally between three groups to find a third of 12.

○ ○ ○ ____

5 Find the fractions of each amount.

a. $\frac{1}{10}$ of 20 = _____   **b.** $\frac{1}{5}$ of 15 = _____   **c.** $\frac{1}{4}$ of 8 = _____

d. $\frac{1}{2}$ of 40 = _____   **e.** $\frac{1}{3}$ of 21 = _____   **f.** $\frac{1}{6}$ of 30 = _____

Apply

6 Solve these problems.

a. A shop sells 20 bags of crisps. $\frac{1}{4}$ of the bags that it sells are salt and vinegar. How many bags of crisps are salt and vinegar? _____

b. There are 30 children in a class. $\frac{1}{3}$ of the class wear glasses. The rest do not wear glasses. How many children do not wear glasses? _____

Equivalent fractions

Remember

A fraction is part of a whole. The bottom number (denominator) shows how many equal parts the whole is split into. The top number (numerator) shows how many of those equal parts are in the fraction.

So, $\frac{1}{4}$ is 1 equal part of a whole split into 4.
$\frac{2}{4}$ are 2 equal parts of a whole split into 4.
Equivalent fractions are fractions that are the same as one another (equal).

This bar model shows how $\frac{1}{2}$ is equal to $\frac{2}{4}$.

$\frac{1}{2}$		$\frac{1}{2}$	
$\frac{1}{4}$	$\frac{1}{4}$	$\frac{1}{4}$	$\frac{1}{4}$

Practise

(1) Circle the letter of the bar that is equivalent to a half.

    A   **B**   **C**   **D**

(2) Here are some cars. Kylie has $\frac{1}{2}$ of the cars. Sophia has $\frac{2}{4}$ of the cars.

  a. Circle Kylie's cars. How many cars does Kylie have? _____

  b. Circle Sophia's cars. How many cars does Sophia have? _____

  c. Complete the sentences.

     Kylie and Sophia both have _____ cars. They have the same number

     because $\frac{1}{2}$ and $\frac{2}{4}$ are _____.

Extend

3 Use the bar model to complete these sentences.

40			
10	10	10	10

a. The whole is equal to _____ .

b. One half is equal to _____ .

c. Two quarters is equal to _____ .

4 Zara has different numbers of counters. She splits them into halves and quarters. She can split 8 counters into both halves and quarters.

$\frac{1}{2}$ of 8 counters is 4.

$\frac{1}{4}$ of 8 counters is 2.

Sort the numbers of counters into the correct place in the Venn diagram. One has been done for you.

| 8̸ | 16 | 6 | 10 | 20 | 9 | 24 |

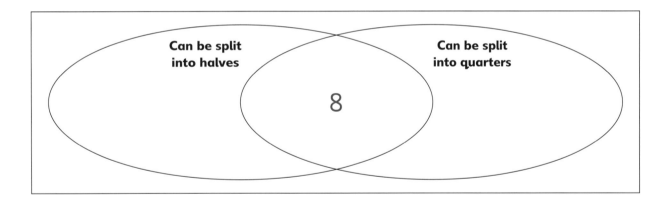

Apply

5 Max has 12 football cards. He gives half of them to Sarah and $\frac{2}{4}$ of them to Raj. Who gets the most cards? Circle **one**.

Sarah   Raj   Neither

Explain your answer.

_____

Length

Remember

Length is the distance from one end of something to the other end. The units used for measuring length are metres (m), centimetres (cm) and millimetres (mm). Always start measuring from 0 on a ruler. For example: the length of this line is 4cm. Check with a ruler. _____

 Practise

1 Write the length of each pencil. Include the correct units.

a.

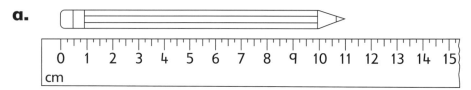

_____

b.

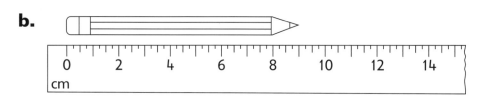

_____

2 Here are some units of measure for length. Write the best unit to measure these items.

| mm | cm | m | km |

a. the height of a house _____

b. the length of a book _____

c. the length of a beetle _____

3 Measure the length of each line in cm using a ruler. Include the correct units.

a. ———————————————— _____

b. ————————————————————— _____

c. ———————————————————— _____

Extend

4 Add these lengths.

   a. 25cm + 4cm = _____ cm   **b.** 43cm + 8cm = _____ cm

   c. 53cm + 32cm = _____ cm   **d.** 48cm + 26cm = _____ cm

5 Subtract these lengths.

   a. 56cm − 5cm = _____ cm   **b.** 82cm − 6cm = _____ cm

   c. 45cm − 13cm = _____ cm   **d.** 74cm − 37cm = _____ cm

 **Apply**

6 Here are two pieces of ribbon.

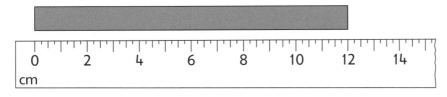

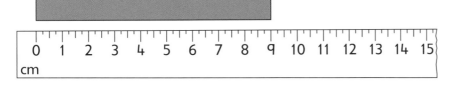

Calculate the difference between the lengths of the ribbon. _____

7 Orla says that the length of this pencil is 12cm long.

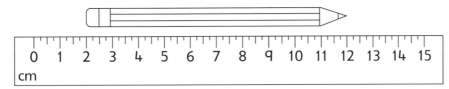

Orla is **not** correct. Explain why.

_____

_____

_____

Mass

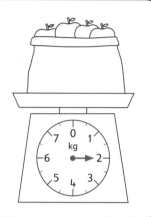
Practise

(1) Complete the sentences.

a. The lightest item is the

_____.

The heaviest item is the _____.

b.

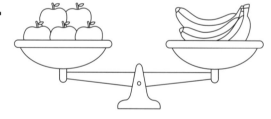 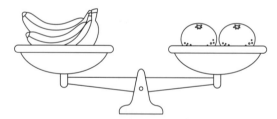

The mass of 2 oranges is the same as _____ apples.

(2) Write the mass of each fruit. Include the correct units.

a.

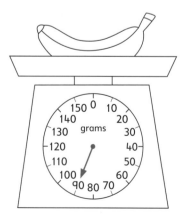

_____

b.

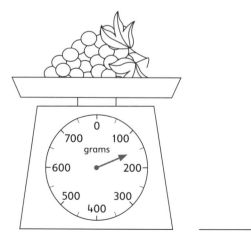

_____

Extend

3 Add these masses.

    a. 43g + 5g = _____ g

    b. 48g + 6g = _____ g

    c. 54kg + 12kg = _____ kg

    d. 37kg + 45kg = _____ kg

4 Subtract these masses.

    a. 67g − 4g = _____ g

    b. 58g − 3g = _____ g

    c. 78kg − 16kg = _____ kg

    d. 83kg − 25kg = _____ kg

5 Here are some bags with different masses.

 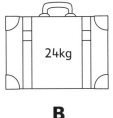   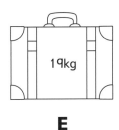

     A   **B**   **C**   **D**   **E**

Write the letters in order from heaviest to lightest.

_____

 Apply

6 Solve these problems.

    a. Calculate the difference between the measurements shown on these two scales.

                                             _____

    b. The mass of a box of books is 28kg. The mass of a box of shoes is 10kg. The mass of a box of toys is 13kg. Calculate the total mass of all three boxes. _____

Capacity

The capacity is the amount of liquid a container holds. The units used most often when measuring capacity are litres (l) and millilitres (ml). There are 1000 millilitres in 1 litre.

Read the scale on the jug at the water level to find out how much liquid it holds. For example: there are 300ml of water in this jug.

Practise

(1) Put the letters of the glasses in order from full to empty.

A   **B**   **C**   **D**   _____

(2) Write the amount of water in each container. Include the correct units.

a.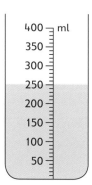
b.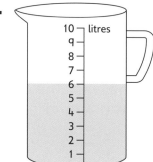

a. _____   **b.** _____   **c.** _____   **d.** _____

(3) Here are some units of measure for capacity. Write the best unit to measure the amount of liquid held by these items.

| ml | l |

a. a spoon _____   **b.** a kettle _____

c. a carton of milk _____   **d.** a can of drink _____

4 Draw a line to show how much water is in each jug.

a.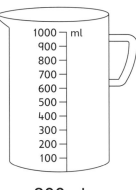

800ml

b.

5 and a half litres

5 Add these capacities.

a. 71ml + 5ml = _____ ml

b. 48ml + 6ml = _____ ml

c. 46ml + 13ml = _____ ml

d. 64ml + 38ml = _____ ml

6 Subtract these capacities.

a. 88ml − 7ml = _____ ml

b. 92ml − 5ml = _____ ml

c. 45l − 12l = _____ l

d. 73l − 24l = _____ l

Apply

7 Here is a jug of water.

a. How much more water needs to be added so that the jug has 100ml?

_____

b. How much water would be in the jug if Alex poured 25ml of water into it?

_____

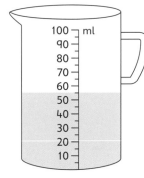

c. How much water would be left in the jug if Erin poured 40ml of water out of it?

_____

Tip Begin by reading the scale on the jug carefully and writing down how much water is in the jug. Use this number for every question.

Time

Practise

1 Draw hands on the clocks to show the times.

a. half past 3

b. 20 minutes to 1

c. 5 minutes past 6

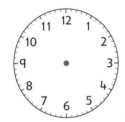  

2 Write the time shown for each activity in words. One has been done for you.

a.

It is ____quarter____

____past 5____.

b.

It is _____

_____.

c.

It is _____

_____.

d.

It is _____

_____.

Extend

3 Complete the part–whole models. One has been done for you.

a.

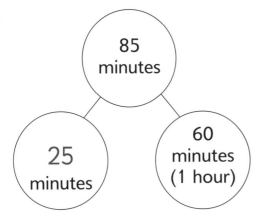

b.

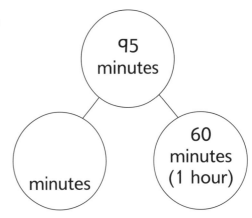

c.

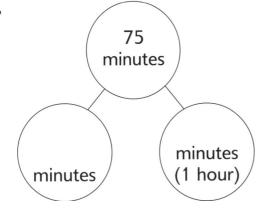

d.

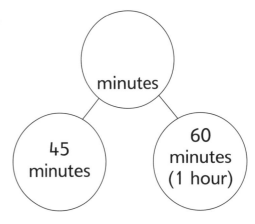

4 This table shows how long some after-school clubs take.

Art	Drama	French	Football
75 minutes	55 minutes	25 minutes	1 hour

Write the names of the clubs in order from shortest to longest time taken.

_____

Apply

5 Heidi starts painting at three o'clock.
She paints for 50 minutes.

  a. Draw the start and end times on the clocks to show how long Heidi is painting.

  b. What time did Heidi finish painting?

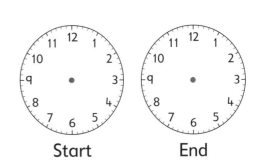

Start   End

_____

Money

Money uses the units £ and pence. 100p = £1. These are the coins used in the money system:

Practise

(1) Draw lines to match the value of each coin to the correct amount.

5p	1p	50p	20p	£1

(2) Emma buys a pencil costing 75p and a rubber costing 32p.

a. Tick the **three** coins that Emma uses to pay for the pencil.

☐ ☐ ☐ ☐ ☐ ☐

b. Tick the **three** coins that Emma uses to pay for the rubber.

☐ ☐ ☐ ☐ ☐ ☐

Unit 4 • **Measurement**

Schofield & Sims

Extend

3 Complete these part–whole models using these coins. You can use the coins more than once.

a.

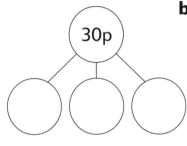

b.

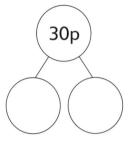

c.

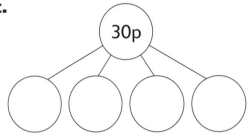

4 Write the correct symbol (<, > or =) in the circle to compare the amounts.

Apply

5 Here are some items for sale at the bakery.

   65p   80p for 2   15p each   90p

a. How much would it cost to buy 1 doughnut? _____

b. Ying buys a fruit tart. She pays for it using a £1 coin. How much change does she get? _____

c. What is the difference between the price of two doughnuts and the price of 1 cupcake? _____

d. Toby spends £1 and 70p. What items could Toby have bought? Give **one** answer.

_____

Temperature

Temperature measures how hot or cold somewhere or something is. The units used for measuring temperature are degrees Celsius (°C).

A thermometer can be used to tell the temperature. This thermometer shows 10°C.

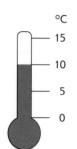

 Practise

1 Choose the best temperature for each picture. Use each temperature once.

5°C	97°C	160°C	32°C

a.

_____

b.

_____

c.

_____

d.

_____

2 Write the temperatures shown on the thermometers.

a.

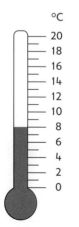

_____

b.

_____

Extend

3 Draw lines to show these temperatures on the thermometers.

a. 10°C

b. 20°C

c. 7°C

 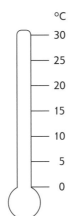 

4 Here is a chart showing the temperature in different cities in the morning and afternoon. In all five cities, the temperature was 5°C hotter in the afternoon than it was in the morning. Complete the table with the missing temperatures.

	City	Morning	Afternoon
a.	London	14°C	
b.	Moscow	8°C	
c.	Sydney	29°C	
d.	Paris		21°C

Apply

5 Mason is cooking in the kitchen with his dad. The thermometer shows the temperature when they start cooking. The temperature rises by 6°C while they are cooking. What is the temperature in the kitchen when they have finished cooking?

_____

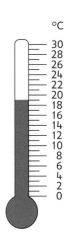

2D shapes

Practise

1 Write the names of these 2D shapes.

a.

_____

b.

_____

c.

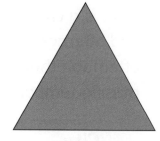

_____

d.

_____

e.

_____

f.

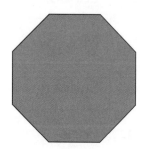

_____

2 Complete the table to show the number of vertices and sides for each shape.

	Shape		Vertices	Sides
a.	Hexagon			
b.	Trapezium			
c.	Kite			

Tip Vertices are the corners of the shape.

(3) Put the letters of the shapes in the correct place on the sorting diagram.

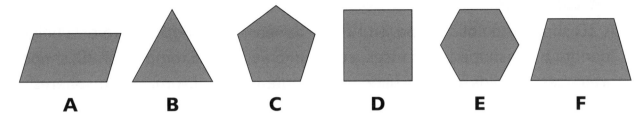

4 sides or fewer	5 sides or more

(4) Tick the pentagons. Tick **more than one**.

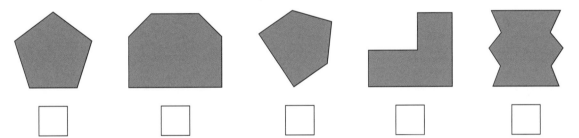

☐	☐	☐	☐	☐

 Apply

(5) Bryn has drawn a picture using 2D shapes. Complete the table to show how many of each shape he has used. One has been done for you.

Shape	Number
circle	2

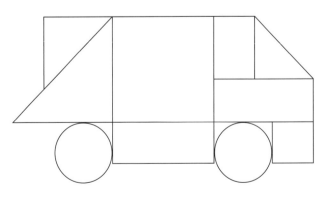

3D shapes

 Practise

(1) Here are some everyday objects put into pairs. Draw lines to match each 3D shape name to the correct pair.

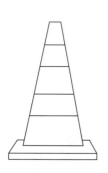 

cylinders

 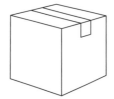

spheres

cubes

cones

2 Complete the table to show the number of faces, vertices and edges for each shape.

	Shape		Faces	Edges	Vertices
a.	Cube	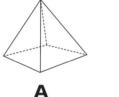			
b.	Square-based pyramid				
c.	Cuboid				

3 Write the letter of each shape in the correct part of the Venn diagram.

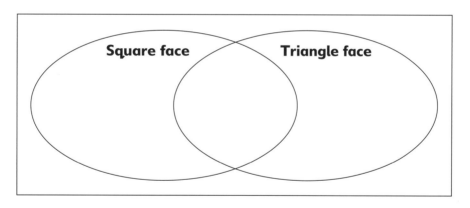

A   **B**   **C**

Square face   Triangle face

4 George wants to make a 3D model of a triangle-based pyramid using spaghetti and marshmallows. He will use spaghetti for the edges of the triangle-based pyramid and marshmallows for the vertices.

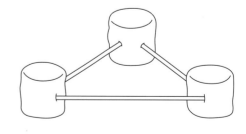

a. How many marshmallows does he need in total? _____

b. How many pieces of spaghetti does he need in total? _____

Lines of symmetry

Remember

A line of symmetry is a line that cuts a shape exactly in half. This means that if the shape was folded along the line, both halves would match exactly. This triangle has one line of symmetry down the middle.

 Practise

1 Draw **one** line of symmetry on each shape.

a.

b.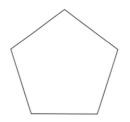

c.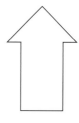

d.

e.

f.

2 Complete the pictures by drawing the other half using the dotted lines.

a.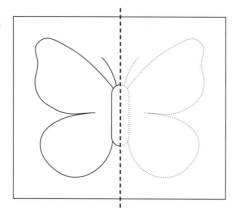

b.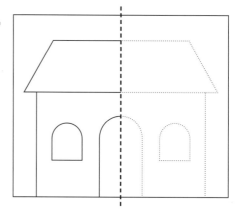

Tip If you put a mirror on the dashed line, the image in the mirror would look exactly the same as your picture.

Extend

3 Draw as many lines of symmetry as possible on this square.

> **Tip** Some shapes, like this square, have more than one line of symmetry. To find other lines of symmetry, think about how the square would look if it was folded from different directions. Remember that you can fold diagonally as well as down the middle.

4 Shade in the squares to complete the symmetrical patterns.

a.

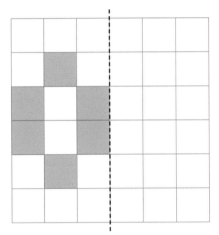

b.

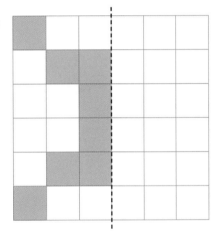

Apply

5 Write each letter in the correct part of the sorting diagram.

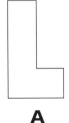

A   **B**   **C**   **D**

	A shape with symmetry	A shape with no symmetry
Has 4 or more sides		
Has fewer than 4 sides		

Patterns

Remember

A pattern is a special order of shapes or numbers. Here is a shape pattern.

The repeated part of the pattern is 2 circles and 1 triangle. It is shown three times here.

Practise

1 Circle the repeated part of each pattern.

a.

b.

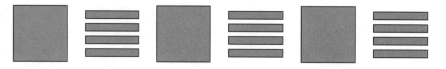

c.

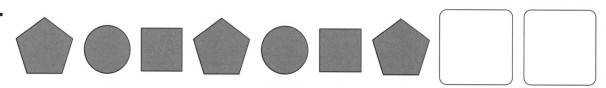

2 Draw the next **two** shapes in each pattern.

a.

b.

c.

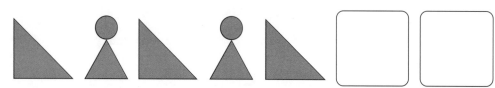

3 Draw the shape that would come tenth in the sequence.

a.

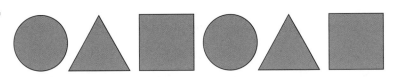

b.

c.

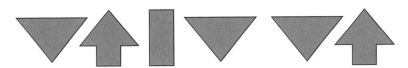

4 Draw the missing shapes in these patterns.

a.

b.

c.

Apply

5 Circle the letter of the card that fits the shape pattern.

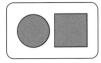

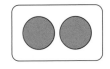

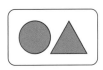

A   **B**   **C**   **D**

Position and turns

There are many different words that describe the position (place) of an object. For example: 'below', 'under', 'next to', 'above' and 'on top of'. Ordinal numbers can also be used to describe position. For example: 'first position'. Always count from the first picture on the left of the sequence to find a picture's position.

An angle is a description of a turn. A turn can be clockwise or anticlockwise. Here the minute hand has moved a quarter turn clockwise between the two clocks.

Practise

1 Hiran is making a jam sandwich. Use the numbers 1, 2, 3 and 4 to show the order of the steps in making the sandwich.

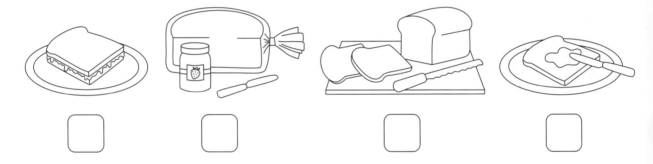

2 Complete these sentences using the words in the box. Use each word or group of words once.

above	next to	under

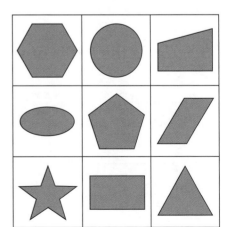

a. The pentagon is _____ the rectangle.

b. The triangle is _____ the parallelogram.

c. The circle is _____ the hexagon.

Extend

3) Tick to show how the pen has moved.

a.

b.

a.
A quarter turn clockwise ☐

A half turn ☐

A quarter turn anticlockwise ☐

b.
A quarter turn clockwise ☐

A half turn ☐

A quarter turn anticlockwise ☐

4) Tick to show whether the statements are true or false.

  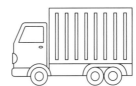

	Statement	True	False
a.	The van is in the second position.		
b.	The car is between the van and lorry.		
c.	The motorbike is behind the lorry.		

Apply

5) **a.** Use the words **forwards**, **turn left** and **turn right** to describe the turtle's journey to the circle.

_____

_____

b. Use the words **forwards**, **turn left** and **turn right** to describe a **different** route back from the circle.

_____

_____

Tally charts

Practise

1 Kai and Amy go on a minibeast hunt. These are the minibeasts they find.

a. Complete the tally chart to show the minibeasts they found.

Minibeast	Tally	Number
Worm		
Bee		
Slug		
Spider		
Woodlouse		

b. How many more slugs than bees were found? _____

c. How many minibeasts were found altogether? _____

Extend

2 The children in Year 2 chose their favourite sports.

a. Complete the table to show their favourite sports.

b. Which sport was the most popular?

_____

c. How many more children chose football than swimming?

_____

Sport	Tally	Number
Football	ⅢⅢ ⅢⅢ ⅢⅢ II	
Tennis		12
Swimming		16
Netball	ⅢⅢ III	
Hockey		4

d. A quarter of the children who chose swimming were boys. How many girls chose swimming? _____

Apply

3 The tally charts show the lunch meals that Class 2A had on Monday and Tuesday.

Monday				Tuesday		
Meal	Tally	Number		Meal	Tally	Number
Hot meal	ⅢⅢ ⅢⅢ ⅢⅢ III			Hot meal	ⅢⅢ ⅢⅢ ⅢⅢ ⅢⅢ I	
Packed lunch		12		Packed lunch		11

a. Complete the tally charts.

b. Calculate the total number of hot meals that Class 2A had on Monday and Tuesday. _____

c. Calculate the difference between the number of children who had a packed lunch on Monday and on Tuesday. _____

d. On Tuesday there were no children absent for lunch. How many children were absent for lunch on Monday? _____

Tables

 Practise

1 This table shows the weather forecast.

Monday	Tuesday	Wednesday	Thursday	Friday	Saturday	Sunday
☀	☀	☁	☀	☀	☀	☀

a. Which day is cloudy? _____

b. How many days are sunny? _____

2 This table shows the number of children that went to four activities at a leisure centre one week in the summer holidays.

Ice skating	Swimming	Basketball	Gymnastics
68	93	74	89

a. How many children went to gymnastics? _____

b. How many more children went swimming than ice skating? _____

c. Basketball had space for 100 children. How many more spaces were available? _____

d. $\frac{1}{2}$ of the children who went ice skating used a skating aid. How many children used a skating aid? _____

3 This table shows the number of visitors to the local farm over the weekend.

a. How many adults and children visited the farm on Sunday?

_____

b. How many children visited the farm on Saturday?

_____

	Saturday	Sunday
Adults	56	39
Children		27
Total	68	

c. How many adults and children visited the farm over the weekend?   _____

 Apply

4 This table describes the reptiles that Maisy saw at the zoo.

Name	Length (metres)	Age (years)	Diet
Iguana	1	4	plants and insects
Python	18	18	animals
Giant tortoise	1	100	plants
Crocodile	5	55	animals

a. What is the diet of a giant tortoise?   _____

b. Which **two** reptiles have the same length?

_____

c. Put the ages of the reptiles in order from youngest to oldest.

_____

d. Calculate the difference between the lengths of the python and the crocodile.   _____

Block charts

A block chart is a type of graph that uses blocks to represent information. The blocks are drawn against two axes. One axis shows what each bar of blocks is showing and the other gives information about the quantities involved.

 Practise

1 Asha collects information about how children in Year 2 travel to school. This table shows the results.

Bus	Car	Train	Cycle	Walk
13	17	4	12	20

a. Complete the block chart to show the results.

b. Which is the most popular way to travel to school? _____

c. Which is the least popular way to travel to school? _____

d. How many more children travel to school by car than cycle? _____

(2) This block chart shows the drinks bought in a café. Use the block chart to complete the sentences.

a. _____ milkshakes were sold.

b. _____ teas and coffees were sold altogether.

c. _____ more glasses of juice than bottles of water were sold.

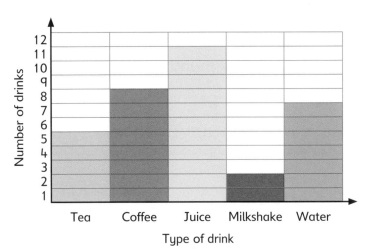

☁ Apply

(3) These block charts show the test marks of pupils in 2G and 2H.

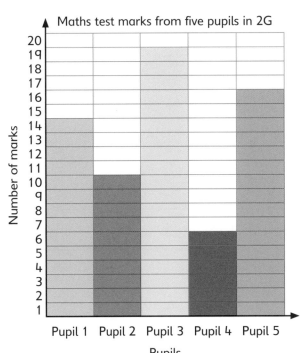

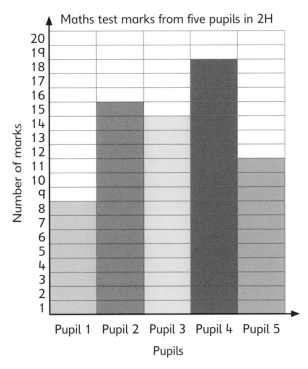

a. How many pupils scored less than 10 marks in class 2G? _____

b. How many pupils scored more than 15 marks in both classes? _____

c. Which pupil, in which class, scored the highest maths test results? _____

Pictograms

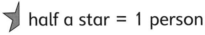
Practise

1. This pictogram shows the number of smoothies that a smoothie stand sells in an hour.

Smoothie	Number sold
Berry	🥤🥤🥤🥤🥤
Apple and orange	🥤🥤🥤🥤🥤🥤🥤🥤
Banana and apple	🥤🥤🥤🥤
Watermelon	🥤🥤🥤🥤🥤

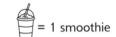 = 1 smoothie

Tip Use the key to find out the number that each symbol represents.

a. How many watermelon smoothies are sold? _____

b. How many smoothies that include apple are sold? _____

c. How many more apple and orange smoothies are sold than berry smoothies? _____

d. What is the total number of smoothies that are sold? _____

e. Calculate the difference between the number of berry smoothies and the number of watermelon smoothies. _____

>> Extend

2 This pictogram shows the number of children who cycle to school each day.

Day	Number of children
Monday	▲ ▲ ▲ ▲ ▲
Tuesday	▲ ▲ ▲ ▲ ▲ ▲
Wednesday	▲ ▲ ▲
Thursday	▲ ▲
Friday	▲ ▲ ▲ ▲

▲ = 5 children

a. What is the total number of children who cycle to school on Monday and Tuesday? _____

b. The school's bike shed can fit 45 bikes. How many more bikes could fit in the shed on Tuesday? _____

Apply

3 This pictogram shows children's birthdays during each of the four seasons.

Season	Spring	Summer	Autumn	Winter
Birthdays	▪ ▪	▪ ▪	▪ ▫	▪

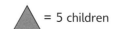 = 8 birthdays

a. Complete the table to show the number of children born in each season.

Season	Number of children born
Spring	
Summer	
Autumn	
Winter	

b. Find the difference between the number of birthdays in summer and the number of birthdays in winter. _____

Final practice

The Final practice assesses knowledge from every unit of this book. Work through the questions carefully and try to answer each one. The target time for completing these questions is 40 minutes. The answers can be downloaded from the **Schofield & Sims** website.

1 Complete the part–whole models.

a.

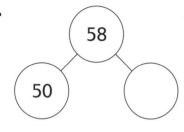

b.

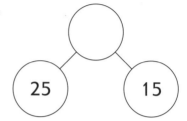

2 marks

2 Write the amounts of money shown.

a.

_____

b.

_____

c.

_____

3 marks

3 Complete the calculations.

a.	4 2	**b.**	7 5	**c.**	8 5	**d.**	6 7
	+ 6 1		+ 4 6		− 3 5		− 4 8

4 marks

4 Write the length of the pencil. Include the correct units.

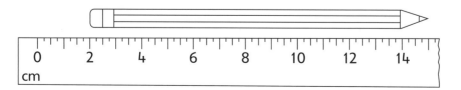

_____

1 mark

Final practice

5 Complete the table to show these words and numerals.

	Words	Numerals
a.	sixteen	
b.		40
c.	eleven	
d.		69
e.	eighty	

5 marks

6 Ayo has £1. How much change would he get if he bought each item?

a.

25p

b.

78p

_____   _____

2 marks

7 Solve these problems.

a. Joe and Rosie are playing a computer game.
Joe scores 78 points and Rosie scores 46 points.
How many points do they score altogether? _____

b. Arnav buys a pair of trainers for £55. Alfie buys
a pair of trainers for £37. What is the difference
between the prices of the two pairs of trainers? _____

4 marks

8 Find the missing digits in these calculations.

a.
```
    6 7
-   3 □
─────────
    3 4
```

b.
```
    8 □
+ □ 5
─────────
  1 7 0
```

c.
```
    8 □
- □ 7
─────────
  2 6
```

5 marks

9 There are 12 cans of cola at a party. $\frac{1}{4}$ of the cans are **not** opened. How many cans of cola are opened? _____

1 mark

10 Here is a pictogram showing the number of letters that were received by the school office in a week.

Days	Number of letters
Monday	✉ ✉
Tuesday	✉ ✉ ✉ ✉
Wednesday	✉ ✉
Thursday	✉ ✉ ✉
Friday	✉

✉ = 10 letters

a. How many letters were received on Monday? _____

b. How many letters were received on Tuesday and Thursday altogether? _____

2 marks

11 Ed circles the letter of the card he thinks is missing from the pattern.

A   **B**   **C**   **D**

Ed is **not** correct. Explain why.

_____

_____

1 mark

Total:

30 marks